This book belongs to:

_____

For Isabelle and Eliza

Text copyright © 2023 by Janet Petrunia
Illustrations copyright © 2023 by Janet Petrunia
Formatted by Eliza Blacquiere

All rights reserved. No part of this publication may be reproduced, distributed, transmitted, or stored in or introduced into a retrieval system, in any form or by any means, graphic, electronic, or mechanical, including photocopying, taping, and recording, or otherwise, without prior written permission from the publisher.

This edition first printing, November 2023

ISBN 978-1-7381459-0-4

Button Books

Prince Edward Island, Canada

Grace's Car Ride

Story and Illustrations by
Janet Petrunia

On a tiny island named for a Prince, there lived a little girl who looked at the world through her imagination. She was brave and bold and adventurous. Her name was Grace, and she could see beauty and fun wherever she looked.

Today Grace and her Mother were taking a long car ride to her Grandmother's house.

Grace loved visiting her Grandmother. She had a large farm with a beautiful pond that shimmered in the sunlight. It was full of colourful fish and hopping frogs.

Grace climbed into their car, buckled her seat belt and rolled down her window. She enjoyed car rides. There were always so many wonderful things to see out a car window.

They drove past a park where children were flying kites. The wind was carrying them up and up, high into the sky. It must be fun to be a kite.

Grace lifted her arms and let the wind blow back her hair. A kite would be the perfect adventure on a warm sunny day like today. She could soar high above the car with the clouds and the seagulls.

Grace lowered her arms and straightened her hair. She was thirsty. She picked up the tumbler of lemonade her Mother had packed for her. Grace loved lemonade. It was a very refreshing drink, especially after a windy flight at the end of a long string.

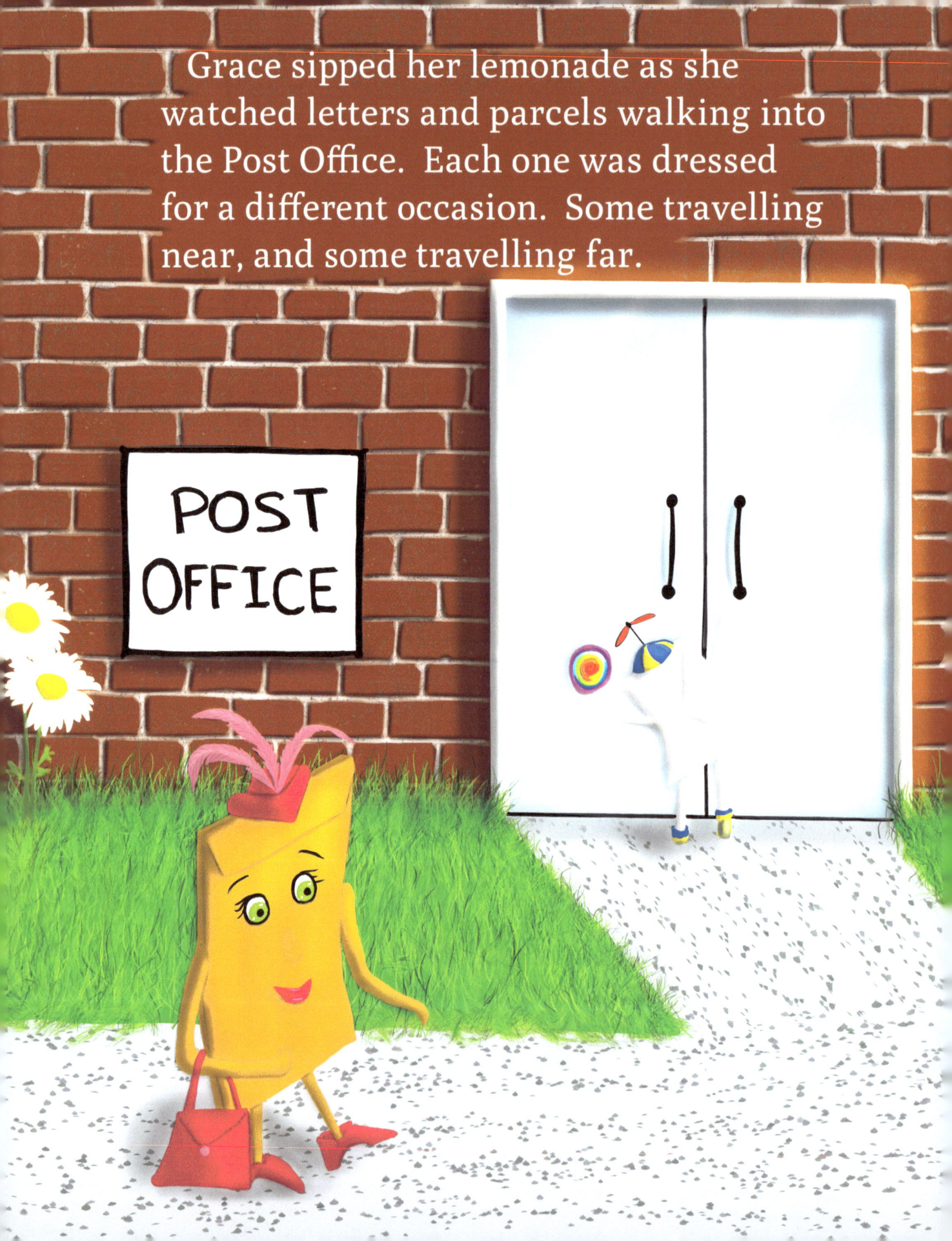

Grace sipped her lemonade as she watched letters and parcels walking into the Post Office. Each one was dressed for a different occasion. Some travelling near, and some travelling far.

Grace returned her tumbler to her cup holder. She looked back out the window in time to see a family of foxes playing hide and seek among the bales in a hay field. Foxes were good at hiding. They could dig out a den under a fallen tree or an old shed. You could walk right past and not even know they were there.

Grace was very good at hide and seek as well. She couldn't dig a den, but she could stay very still and not make a sound.

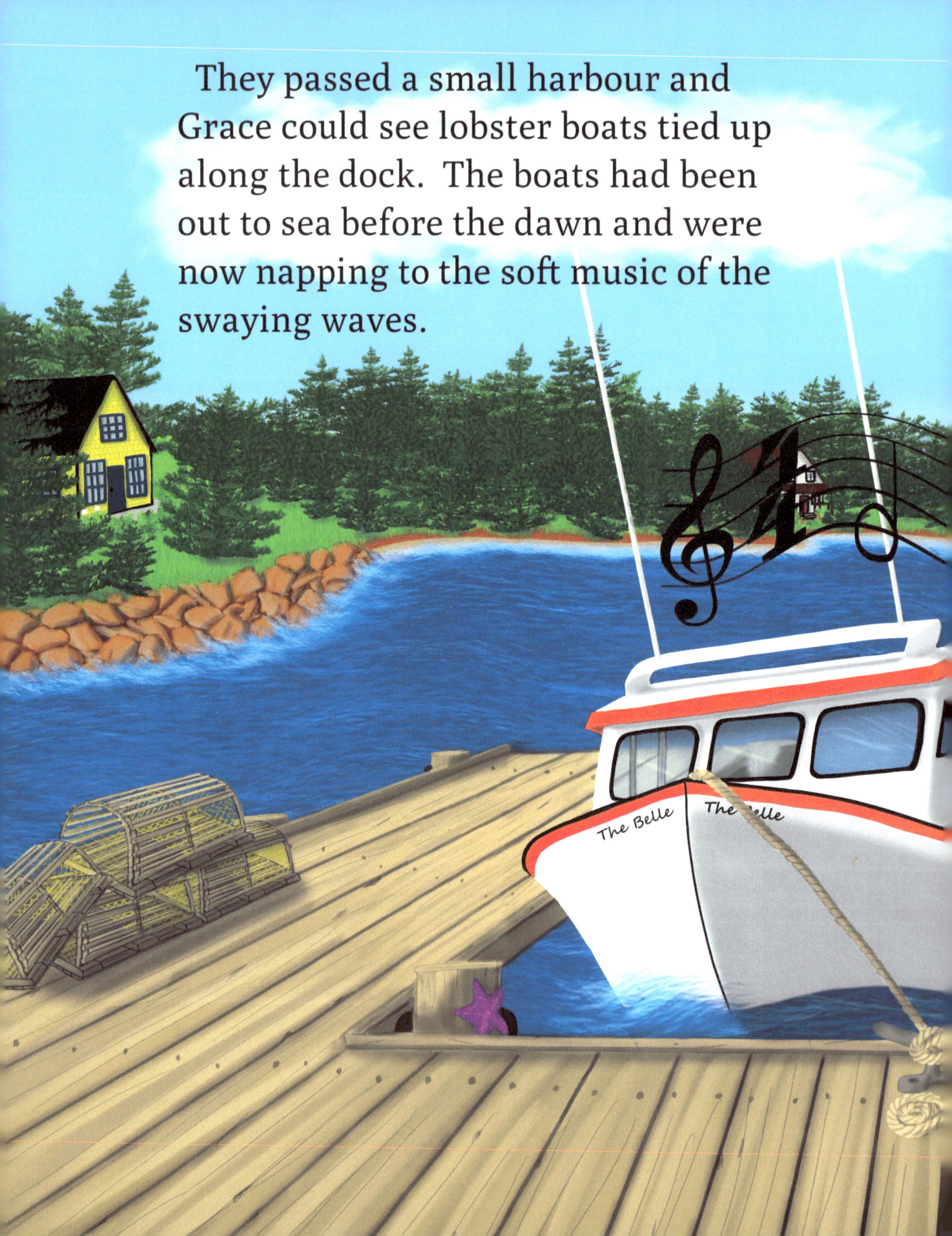

They passed a small harbour and Grace could see lobster boats tied up along the dock. The boats had been out to sea before the dawn and were now napping to the soft music of the swaying waves.

As they drove alongside the beach, Grace spotted a little rowboat waiting on the sand.

She wondered who captained the small boat, and how good a fisherman they might be.

Grace was confident she would make a very good captain. Standing at the helm with the salty wind on her face and the spray of the sea in her hair. She would be guided by dolphins and visited by whales.

Grace caught sight of the large chestnut tree that marked the beginning of her Grandmother's driveway.

As they drove down the long driveway, that Grace was sure could land planes, she spotted her Grandmother waving from the front porch.

Grace loved her Grandmother. She gave Grace hugs that were warmer than the sun.

What do you Imagine...

www.ingramcontent.com/pod-product-compliance
Lightning Source LLC
LaVergne TN
LVHW072057070426
835508LV00002B/145